THE POET'S
TOOLBOX

Cobwebs, Chatters, and Chills

A Collection of Scary Poems

Compiled and Annotated
by Patricia M. Stockland

Illustrated by
Sara Rojo Pérez

Compass Point Books
3109 West 50th Street, #115
Minneapolis, MN 55410

Visit Compass Point Books on the Internet at *www.compasspointbooks.com*
or e-mail your request to *custserv@compasspointbooks.com*

Permissions and Acknowledgements:
"Monday's Troll," 6. Text copyright © 1996 by Jack Prelutsky. Used by permission of HarperCollins Publishers. "I Am Not Scared," 7. Printed by permission of Patricia M. Stockland. "The Witches' Ride," 8. Copyright © 1964, renewed 1992 by Karla Kuskin. Reprinted by permission of S©ott Treimel NY. "Owl," 9. Every effort has been made to contact the author. Compass Point Books does not take credit for the authorship, ownership, or copyright of this poem. "The Troll," 10. Text © 1976 Jack Prelutsky. Used by permission of HarperCollins Publishers. "The Wendigo," 11. Copyright © 1953 by Ogden Nash, renewed. Reprinted by permission of Curtis Brown, Ltd. "The Hidebehind," 12. Reprinted by permission of PFD on behalf of: Michael Rosen © 1974, Michael Rosen: as printed in the original volume. "Strange Tree," 13. Every effort has been made to contact the author. Compass Point Books does not take credit for the authorship, ownership, or copyright of this poem. "Little Orphant Annie," 14-15. Public domain. "I am afraid," 16. SONGS OF THE DREAM PEOPLE: Chants and Images from the Indians and Eskimos of North America. Edited and illustrated by James Houston. Atheneum, New York, copyright © 1972 by James Houston. "When I Was Lost," 17. "When I Was Lost," from ALL TOGETHER by Dorothy Aldis, copyright 1925-1928, 1934, 1939, 1952, renewed 1953, © 1954-1956, 1962 by Dorothy Aldis, © 1967 by Roy E. Porter, renewed. Used by permission of G.P. Putnam's Sons, an imprint of Penguin Putnam Books for Young Readers, a division of Penguin Putnam Inc. All rights reserved. "rollercoaster," 18. "roller coaster" from PEACOCK AND OTHER POEMS by Valerie Worth. Copyright © 2002 Valerie Worth. "Child Frightened by a Thunderstorm," 19. From OFFICIAL ENTRY BLANK, University of Nebraska Press, 1969. Reprinted by permission of the author. "The Bat," 20. "The Bat," copyright 1938 by Theodore Roethke, from THE COLLECTED POEMS OF THEODORE ROETHKE by Theodore Roethke. Used by permission of Doubleday, a division of Random House, Inc. "Monster Mothers," 21. Copyright © 1992 by Florence Parry Heide. First appeared in Grim and Ghastly Goings On, published by Lothrop Lee & Shepard. Reprinted by permission of Curtis Brown, Ltd. "deep in a windless wood," 22. From MORE CRICKET SONGS Japanese haiku translated by Harry Behn. Copyright © 1971 Harry Behn. © Renewed 1999 Prescott Behn, Pamela Behn Adam, and Peter Behn. Used by permission of Marian Reiner. "A Silly Young Fellow Named Hyde," 23. Public domain. "I Don't Believe in Bigfoot," 24. Text copyright © 1996 by Eileen Spinelli from Where Is the Night Train Going? by Eileen Spinelli. Published by Wordsong, Boyds Mills Press, Inc. Reprinted by permission. "That Old Haunted House," 25. Reprinted with the permission of Atheneum Books for Young Readers, an imprint of Simon & Schuster Children's Publishing Division from SAD UNDERWEAR AND OTHER COMPLICATIONS by Judith Viorst. Text copyright © 1995 Judith Viorst.

Content Advisers: Jane K. Volkman, Patricia Kirkpatrick, Ph.D.
Rights Researcher: Nancy Loewen
Designer: The Design Lab

Library of Congress Cataloging-in-Publication Data
Cobwebs, chatters, and chills : a collection of scary poems / compiled and annotated by Patricia M. Stockland.
     p. cm. — (The poet's toolbox)
Summary: An anthology of poems about frightening things, plus "Toolbox tips" that help the reader understand poetry and how poems are written.
ISBN 0-7565-0565-8 (hardcover)
1. Supernatural—Juvenile poetry. 2. Poetry—Authorship—Juvenile literature. 3. Children's poetry, American. 4. Monsters—Juvenile poetry. 5. Horror—Juvenile poetry. 6. Fear—Juvenile poetry. (1. Supernatural—Poetry. 2. Monsters—Poetry. 3. Horror—Poetry. 4. Fear—Poetry. 5. American poetry.) I. Stockland, Patricia M. II. Title. III. Series.
PS595.S94C63 2004
808.81'937—dc22   2003017106

A special thank you to John, Elizabeth, and Chaneen

Table of Contents

4   Open Your Toolbox

6   Poems

26   Collect Your Tools

27   Go to Work

28   The Poet's Toolbox Glossary

30   Finding More Poetry

32   Index

NOTE: In this book, words that are defined in the glossary are in **bold** the first time they appear in the text.

Open Your Toolbox

You've probably been frightened before. Sometimes, everyday stuff can be creepy, like getting lost or being alone. But admit it: there are times when make-believe stuff seems real . . . and terrifying! How do you tell someone about those moments—when an old, gnarled tree looks at you strangely, or the sound of an owl creeps into your dreams, or you're at the top of a roller coaster and your stomach drops to your toes? Poetry can be a way to describe those things—haunted houses, trolls, monsters, bats, roller coasters, thunderstorms, goblins, Bigfoot . . . anything!

WHAT DOES POETRY DO?

Poetry helps energize your imagination. Poetry plays with words in ways you never imagined. Ordinary words become suddenly mysterious or exciting. Poetry opens your ears to different sounds—sentences can play like music. Everyone has smart ideas, and poetry can be a new language with which to share those ideas.

DOES A POET USE A TOOLBOX?

Poets use many different tools and materials to build their poems. Stuff that happens to poets every day in their lives can become material. Poets' tools are parts of speech (such as nouns, verbs, and adjectives), ways of writing (like different forms or types of poetry), and the interesting sounds that letters and words make when they're combined (like rhymes and repeated letters). This book will show you some different tools poets use to create poems, and it might even teach you to write some poetry.

HOW DOES THE POET'S TOOLBOX WORK?

First, read all the poems. After you read each one, take a look at the Toolbox Tip on the bottom of the page. These Toolbox Tips will help you understand a poetry tool the writer has used, or they might give you a hint about where the poet found the idea for that poem. Near the back of the book, you'll have the chance to begin using these tools yourself!

Monday's Troll

Monday's troll is mean and rotten,
Tuesday's troll is misbegotten,
Wednesday's troll is extra smelly,
Thursday's has a baggy belly.

Friday's troll is great and grimy,
Saturday's is short and slimy—
But Sunday's troll is crabby, cross,
And full of sour applesauce.

—Jack Prelutsky

TOOLBOX TIP

RHYME TIME

When words end in the same sound, they **rhyme.** There are a lot of rhymes in this poem. Can you find all of them?

If

Anything
Might

Nudge me in the night
Or
Tickle my uncovered toe,

Scream, I will not,
'Cause I am not scared,
And I
Run faster than
Everything I know, even
Dragons and monsters and shadows!

—Patricia M. Stockland

HIDDEN MESSAGES

TOOLBOX TIP

An **acrostic** poem talks to you in more than one direction. When the first letter of each line is put together, it spells another word or phrase. Sometimes that hidden message is the main idea or title of the poem. What's hidden in this acrostic poem?

The Witches' Ride

Over the hills
Where the edge of the light
Deepens and darkens
To ebony night,
Narrow hats high
Above yellow bead eyes,
The tatter-haired witches
Ride through the skies.
Over the seas
Where the flat fishes sleep
Wrapped in the slap of the slippery deep,
Over the peaks
Where the black trees are bare,
Where boney birds quiver
They glide through the air.
Silently humming
A horrible tune,
They sweep through the stillness
To sit on the moon.

—Karla Kuskin

Music to my ears

TOOLBOX TIP

MUSIC TO MY EARS
The **rhythm** in these poems creates some great beats. In fact, they almost sound like songs. Syllables and rhymes help make rhythm. Tap out the beat with your foot, or sing these poems!

Owl

On Midsummer night the witches shriek,
The frightened fairies swoon,
The nightjar mutters in his sleep
And ghosts around the chimney creep.
The loud winds cry, the fir trees crash,
And the owl stares at the moon.

—Sylvia Read

Measuring meter

MEASURING METER

Did you know rhythm is measured in **meter?** Just count the number of
beats in each line. Some poems always have the same meter in each line.
Others change meter. Which does this poem do?

Gobble! Gobble! Gulp!

The Troll

Be wary of the loathsome troll
that slyly lies in wait
to drag you to his dingy hole
and put you on his plate.

His blood is black and boiling hot,
he gurgles ghastly groans.
He'll cook you in his dinner pot,
your skin, your flesh, your bones.

He'll catch your arms and clutch your legs
and grind you to a pulp,
then swallow you like scrambled eggs—
gobble! gobble! gulp!

So watch your steps when next you go
upon a pleasant stroll,
or you might end in the pit below
as supper for the troll.

—Jack Prelutsky

TOOLBOX TIP

GOBBLE! GOBBLE! GULP!

Do some of these words seem more like sounds than words? That's called **onomatopoeia** (ON-o-MA-tow-PEE-ya)—when a word describes the sound of an action. "Gulp" is an onomatopoeia word. Words like "buzz," "hiss," and "boom" are, too. Can you think of more?

The Wendigo

The Wendigo,
The Wendigo!
Its eyes are ice and indigo!
Its blood is rank and yellowish!
Its voice is hoarse and bellowish!
Its tentacles are slithery,
And scummy,
Slimy,
Leathery!
Its lips are hungry blubbery,
And smacky,
Sucky,
Rubbery!

The Wendigo,
The Wendigo!
I saw it just a friend ago!
Last night it lurked in Canada;
Tonight, on your veranada!
As you are lolling hammockwise
It contemplates you stomachwise.
You loll,
It contemplates,
It lollops.
The rest is merely gulps and gollops.

—Ogden Nash

TOOLBOX TIP

REAL OR MAKE-BELIEVE?
Do you ever make up words? Poets do, and this poet's pretend
word becomes a pretend beast. It might scare you to pieces or
make you laugh. Poetry can make you feel many different things.

The Hidebehind

Have you seen the Hidebehind?
I don't think you will, mind you,
because as you're running through the dark
the Hidebehind's behind you.

—Michael Rosen

WHAT'S THAT? WHO'S THERE?
Have you ever had the feeling that someone—or something—is behind you? Some of the spookiest poems work because they re-create the feeling you get when your brain tricks you into imagining things.

Strange Tree

Away beyond the Jarboe house
I saw a different kind of tree.
Its trunk was old and large and bent,
And I could feel it look at me.

The road was going on and on
Beyond to reach some other place.
I saw a tree that looked at me
And yet it did not have a face.

It looked at me with all its limbs;
It looked at me with all its bark.
The yellow wrinkles on its sides
Were bent and dark.

And then I ran to get away,
But when I stopped to turn and see,
The tree was bending to the side
And leaning out to look at me.

—Elizabeth Madox Roberts

ARE YOU LOOKING AT ME?
TOOLBOX TIP
A tree can't really look at you . . . or can it? Poets can give human traits, or features, to something that isn't human and make it come to life. This is called **personification.**

13

Little Orphant Annie

Little Orphant Annie's come to our house to stay,
An' wash the cups and saucers up, an' brush the crumbs away,
An' shoo the chickens off the porch, an' dust the hearth, an' sweep,
An' make the fire, an' bake the bread, an' earn her board-an'-keep;
An' all us other children, when the supper things is done,
We set around the kitchen fire an' has the mostest fun
A-lis'nin' to the witch-tales 'at Annie tells about,
An' the Gobble-uns 'at gits you
                    Ef you—Don't—Watch—Out!

Onc't they was a little boy wouldn't say his pray'rs—
An' when he went to bed at night, away up stairs,
His mammy heered him holler, an' his daddy heard him bawl,
An' when they turn't the kivvers down, he wasn't there at all!
An' seeked him up the chimney-flue, an' ever'wheres, I guess;
But all they ever found was thist his pants an' round-about!
An' the Gobble-uns 'll git you
                    Ef you—Don't—Watch—Out!

Crazy talk

An' one time a little girl 'ud allus laugh an' grin,
An' make fun of ever'one, an' all her blood-an'-kin;
An' onc't when they was "company," an' ole folks was there,
She mocked 'em an' shocked 'em, an' said she didn't care!
An' thist as she kicked her heels, an' turn't to run an' hide,
They was two great big Black Things a-standin' by her side,
An' they snatched her through the ceilin' 'fore she knowed
   what she's about!
An' the Gobble-uns 'll git you

                Ef you—Don't—Watch—Out!

An' little Orphant Annie says, when the blaze is blue,
An' the lampwick sputters, an' the wind goes woo-oo!
An' you hear the crickets quit, an' the moon is gray,
An' the lightnin'-bugs in dew is all squenched away—
You better mind yer parents, and yer teachers fond and dear,
An' cherish them 'at loves you, an' dry the orphant's tear,
An' he'p the pore an' needy ones 'at clusters all about,
Er the Gobble-uns 'll git you

                Ef you—
                    Don't—
                        Watch—
                          Out!

—James Whitcomb Riley

CRAZY TALK

TOOLBOX TIP This poet left a lot of letters out of words. At first, the words might read like nonsense. Read the poem again aloud, and sound out each word. Does it sound like someone speaking with an accent? Does it help you picture who is speaking?

Untitled

I am afraid
When my eyes follow the moon
On its old trail.
I am afraid
When I hear the wind wailing
And the murmuring of snow.
I am afraid
When I watch the stars
Moving on their nightly trail.
I am afraid.

—Eastern Inuit

Again, and again, and again . . .

TOOLBOX TIP

AGAIN, AND AGAIN, AND AGAIN . . .
You've probably heard an echo. They can be haunting. Sometimes poets use **repetition** to make a point. Repeating lines or words also helps others remember the point.

When I Was Lost

Underneath my belt
My stomach was a stone.
Sinking was the way I felt.
And hollow.
And alone.

—Dorothy Aldis

TOOLBOX TIP

ALL ALONE IN LINES AND RHYMES
Being alone can be frightening! The feeling can kind of creep up on you.
The last line and rhyme in this poem creep up on you, too. Sometimes a poet
will put a rhyming line where you don't expect it to give it more impact.

roller coaster

The sluggish
Clattering
Climb, the
Crest, then
Everything
Falls away:

Nothing
Mattering
But the
Wrenching
Track, the
Hurtling car,

The fingers
Clenched
Like death
On the
Slippery
Safety bar.

—Valerie Worth

Read it . . . feel it

TOOLBOX TIP

READ IT . . . FEEL IT

Imagery is the picture you get in your mind when you read a poem.
Vivid words like "clattering," "wrenching," and "hurtling" all create imagery.
At the end of this poem, do you feel like you are on a roller coaster?

Child Frightened by a Thunderstorm

Thunder has nested in the grass all night
and rumpled it, and with its outstretched wings
has crushed the peonies. Its beak was bright,
sharper than garden shears and, clattering,
it snipped bouquets of branches for its bed.
I could not sleep. The thunder's eyes were red.

—Ted Kooser

What's in there?

TOOLBOX TIP

WHAT'S IN THERE?
This poem uses a **metaphor** of a large, frightening bird to show what thunder is like. Metaphors give the qualities of one thing to something else. Poets can suggest new ideas with metaphors. Although thunder doesn't really have wings or a beak, what could the poet mean?

19

The Bat

By day the bat is cousin to the mouse.
He likes the attic of an aging house.

His fingers make a hat about his head.
His pulse beat is so slow we think him dead.

He loops in crazy figures half the night
Among the trees that face the corner light.

But when he brushes up against a screen,
We are afraid of what our eyes have seen:

For something is amiss or out of place
When mice with wings can wear a human face.

—Theodore Roethke

TOOLBOX TIP

TAKE TWO
The meter in this poem is nice and even—every line has 10 beats. When
a poet groups two even lines of poetry, it is called a **couplet.** The
lines usually rhyme, and each couplet makes its own image or point.

Monster Mothers

When monster mothers get together
they brag about their babies.
The other day I heard one say,
"He got his very first fang today!"

"Mine is ugly."
"Mine is mean."
"Mine is turning
 nice and green."

"Mine's as scaly
 as a fish."
"Mine is sort of
 yellowish."

"Mine breathes fire
 and smoke and such."
"Mine has skin
 you'd hate to touch."

—Florence Parry Heide

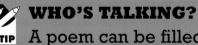

WHO'S TALKING?
A poem can be filled with many
voices. How many monster mothers
could be talking in this poem?

Can you haiku?

Untitled

Deep in a windless
wood, not one leaf dares to move . . . .
Something is afraid.

—Buson

Translated from Japanese by Harry Behn

CAN YOU HAIKU?

TOOLBOX TIP This poet captured the creepy feeling of complete silence and stillness in three lines! This Japanese form of poetry is **haiku.** It doesn't rhyme, but it always has the same number of beats—17 total. How many are in each line?

22

A Silly Young Fellow Named Hyde

A silly young fellow named Hyde
In a funeral procession was spied;
    When asked, "Who is dead?"
    He giggled and said,
"I don't know, I just came for the ride."

—Author Unknown

TOOLBOX TIP

A NEAT TRICK CALLED LIMERICK
A **limerick** is a funny poem with five lines. The first, second, and last lines rhyme. The third and fourth lines are shorter and rhyme with each other. Do you think this limerick really happened?

I Don't Believe in Bigfoot

I don't believe in Bigfoot
Or skeletons that dance.
I don't believe in werewolves
Or zombies in a trance.
I don't believe in Martians
Or ghosts in sheets of white.
I don't believe in witches,
Who ride their brooms at night.
I don't believe in vampires
Or monsters from the sea—
And I'm hoping with my fingers crossed
They don't believe in me.

—Eileen Spinelli

TOOLBOX TIP

SAYING WHAT YOU MEAN
When the speaker repeats "I don't believe in," do you think he or she is telling the truth? How do the last two lines reveal the speaker's *true* feelings?

That Old Haunted House

That old haunted house was so creepy, so crawly,
    so ghastly, so ghostly, so gruesome, so skully-and-bony.
That old haunted house gave me nightmares and daymares
    and shudders and shivers and quivers and quavers and quakes.
That old haunted house made my hair stand on end and my
    heart pound-pound-pound and the blood in my veins ice-
    cold-freezing.
That old haunted house gave me goose bumps and throat lumps
    and ch-ch-ch-chattering teeth and the sh-sh-sh-shakes.
That old haunted house made me shriek, made me eeek, made
    me faint, made me scared-to-death scared, made me all-over
    sweat.
Would I ever go back to that old haunted house?
You bet.

—Judith Viorst

TOOLBOX TIP

CREAKS AND CHILLS

Describe the scariest thing that's ever happened to you.
Is it hard to put into words? Does stretching or combining
words help? That's what this poet has done.

Poets use a lot of tools to build their poems. What poetry tools have you learned in reading this book? When you find the answers to the questions on these pages, you're learning to work just like a poet. (Hint: Need help with a word you don't understand? Look in The Poet's Toolbox Glossary on page 28.)

1. When words end in the same sound, they often **rhyme,** such as the poem "Monday's Troll" on page 6. Find other poems that have rhyming lines. Do the rhymes always appear in the same pattern?

2. On page 16, the Eastern Inuit poem repeats the phrase "I am afraid." Can you find other poems that use the tool of **repetition?**

3. In "Little Orphant Annie" (page 14), James Whitcomb Riley separates groups of lines and ideas with **stanzas.** Find other poems that use stanzas.

4. You can get a good picture of a poem because of **imagery.** Poets create imagery by using a lot of details. Which poems created good pictures in your mind? What were some of the details in those poems?

5. You read in "Child Frightened by a Thunderstorm" (page 19) that thunder can have wings, a beak, and red eyes because of **metaphor.** Find another poem that uses metaphor to help describe something.

Congratulations! Now you know a whole lot more about the tools poets use, and you're probably able to use some of these tools yourself. You've seen lots of examples. Now go to the next page, and get out your pencil and paper. It's time to build your own poems!

You know how to use some poetry tools, so it's time to go to work. Here's an activity that will help you get going on writing some of your own poems.

MAKE YOUR OWN POETRY BOOK

Write a book of poems about things that scare you.

1. Get a notebook. It can be a plain old notebook, nothing fancy.

2. Make a list of things that scare you or your friends. If you want, use some of the words or ideas you found in this book.
   - Are you afraid of the dark?
   - Do you believe in monsters, trolls, ghosts, or goblins?
   - Have you ever heard creepy sounds?
   - Have you ever been lost or alone?
   - Have you ever seen a haunted house?
   - Do you know any ghost stories?
   - Have you ever been in a forest of scary trees?

3. Look at the poet's tools you collected on the previous page. Try using some of those tools to turn your list into poems. You could write an acrostic poem about ghosts. Just turn to page 7 for an example. Page 20 might help if you want to write a rhyming poem or use couplets.

4. Now, make your poetry book. Read back over what you've written. Choose five poems that you really like. Copy these five poems on to fresh sheets of paper. Draw pictures to match your poems. Staple these pages together, and you have your own poetry book!

Go to Work

The Poet's Toolbox Glossary can help you understand poetry tools used in this book and others in this series. Words in **color** are tools found in this book. Words in **black** are other poetry tools that will also be helpful as you work on your own poetry.

Alliteration (ah-LIT-er-A-shun) is a tool that helps with sounds. It repeats consonant sounds or vowel sounds that are the same, like the "m" in "marvelous malted milk" or the "o" sound in "Go home, Joe."

Acrostic poems use the first letters of each line to spell out a word, name, or phrase relating to the poem's topic.

Comparing and contrasting helps you to see what is the same or different about two or more ideas, objects, people, places, or anything. For example, a poet might compare an old shoe to a new shoe by listing the way the two shoes smell (stinky or fresh), look (dirty or clean), and feel (comfortable or stiff).

Concrete poems look like something you can touch. The way words and lines are arranged on the page is just as important as what they mean. A poem about the sun might be round like the sun, or a poem about a swing might look like the words are swinging.

Couplets are pairs of rhyming lines that usually have the same number of beats. Couplets make their own point, create a separate image, or summarize the idea of a poem.

Free verse poetry is poetry that doesn't have to rhyme or stay in stanzas, or even lines. Don't let the word "free" trick you, though. The poet might use other tools to keep the poem tied together, like repeating the same sounds or words.

Haiku usually has 17 syllables (or beats) in three lines—five syllables in the first and last lines and seven in the middle. A haiku is a short poem, usually about nature and the seasons.

Imagery is what you see in your mind when you read a poem. Details like colors, sounds, sizes, shapes, comparisons, smells, and flavors all help create imagery.

Limericks are humorous poems with five lines. The last words of the first, second, and fifth lines rhyme, as do the last words of the shorter third and fourth lines. The shorter lines have two stressed beats, and the longer lines have three stressed beats.

Metaphors show how two different things are similar by calling one thing something else, such as if you call clouds "balls of cotton."

Meter measures the number of syllables, or beats, in each line of a poem. If you can count the beats, you can determine the meter. For example, some types of poems always have 10 beats per line. Others have 12.

Onomatopoeia (ON-o-MA-tow-PEE-ya) is another cool word tool that poets use. This is when the word suggests the sound or action it means, like "buzz," "hiss," and "boom."

Patterns are several things that are repeated in the same way several times. Many poems create a pattern by repeating rhyming words at the end of each line.

Personification gives human characteristics, or traits, to something that isn't human. It makes an object or animal seem human or come to life.

Repetition is what happens when poets repeat things. Repetition can help create patterns. It can also help make or emphasize a point.

Rhymes are words that end in the same sound. For example, "clock" rhymes with "dock." Rhyming sounds don't have to be spelled the same way. "Pest" rhymes with "dressed."

Rhythm is the beat you can feel in poetry, like a tempo in music. Syllables, or beats, help create rhythm. Rhymes can create rhythm, too. You can measure rhythm through meter.

Similes are comparisons using "as" or "like." When you use a simile, you are saying that one thing is similar to another. Similes can help you create personification. They are also a lot like metaphors.

Stanzas are like paragraphs for poetry. They are groups of lines that sit together and are usually separated by a blank line. Sometimes a poet begins a new thought in a new stanza.

Structure is how a poem was built. A poet can build a poem using lines and stanzas.

Synonyms are words that mean almost the same thing.

Translated means that the poem was originally written in a different language.

Voice is the speaker in a poem. It can be one person, or a bunch of different people. It can be animals, objects, or even the poet.

AT THE LIBRARY

Alarcón, Francisco X. Illustrated by Maya Christina Gonzalez. *From the Bellybutton of the Moon and Other Summer Poems.* San Francisco: Children's Book Press, 1998.

Hughes, Langston. Illustrated by Brian Pinkney. *The Dream Keeper and Other Poems.* New York: Knopf, 1994.

Kennedy, X.J. Illustrated by Joy Allen. *Exploding Gravy: Poems to Make You Laugh.* Boston: Little, Brown, 2002.

Lansky, Bruce. Illustrated by Stephen Carpenter. *If Pigs Could Fly—And Other Deep Thoughts: A Collection of Funny Poems.* Minnetonka, Minn.: Meadowbrook Press, 2000.

Shapiro, Karen Jo. Illustrated by Matt Faulkner. *Because I Could Not Stop My Bike, and Other Poems.* Watertown, Mass.: Whispering Coyote, 2003.

Silverstein, Shel. *Falling Up: Poems and Drawings.* New York: HarperCollins, 1996.

Wong, Janet S. *A Suitcase of Seaweed, and Other Poems.* New York: Margaret K. McElderry Books, 1996.

ON THE ROAD

Riley Museum

528 Lockerbie St.

Indianapolis, IN 46202

317/631-5885

To visit the historical Victorian home of poet

James Whitcomb Riley

WEB SITES

For more information on **poetry,** use FactHound
to track down Web sites related to this book.

1. Go to *www.compasspointbooks.com/facthound*

2. Type in this book ID: **0756505658**

3. Click on the FETCH IT button.

Your trusty FactHound will fetch the best Web sites for you!

ABOUT THE AUTHOR

Patricia M. Stockland has a Bachelor of Arts degree in English from South Dakota State University. She lives in Minnesota and is currently completing her Master of Arts thesis in literature from Minnesota State University, Mankato. She has taught composition and enjoys both writing and helping others write. Patricia is an editor and author of children's nonfiction books.

ABOUT THE ILLUSTRATOR

Sara Rojo Pérez was born in Madrid and now lives in Cádiz on the southern coast of Spain. For many years she worked as the creative director of an animation studio, creating both films and advertisements. Sara works in many different media—from paint in oils or acrylics to computer illustration to sculptures and tapestries. In addition to her artwork, Sara enjoys horseback riding and reading fantasy and mystery novels.

INDEX

"The Bat" (Theodore Roethke), 20

"Child Frightened by a Thunderstorm" (Ted Kooser), 19

"The Hidebehind" (Michael Rosen), 12

"I Am Not Scared" (Patricia M. Stockland), 7
"I Don't Believe in Bigfoot" (Eileen Spinelli), 24

"Little Orphant Annie" (James Whitcomb Riley), 14-15

"Monday's Troll" (Jack Prelutsky), 6
"Monster Mothers" (Florence Parry Heide), 21

"Owl" (Sylvia Read), 9

"roller coaster" (Valerie Worth), 18

"A Silly Young Fellow Named Hyde" (Author Unknown), 23
"Strange Tree" (Elizabeth Madox Roberts), 13

"That Old Haunted House" (Judith Viorst), 25
"The Troll" (Jack Prelutsky), 10

"Untitled" (Buson), 22
"Untitled" (Eastern Inuit), 16

"The Wendigo" (Ogden Nash), 11
"When I Was Lost" (Dorothy Aldis), 17
"The Witches Ride" (Karla Kuskin), 8